Find Your Happy!

7 Observations from the Planet on being Happy.

Constance Stoner

BALBOA.
PRESS

A DIVISION OF HAY HOUSE

Interior Graphics/Art Credit: Constance Grace Stoner

Balboa Press books may be ordered through booksellers or by contacting:

Balboa Press
A Division of Hay House
1663 Liberty Drive
Bloomington, IN 47403
www.balboapress.com
1 (877) 407-4847

Because of the dynamic nature of the Internet, any web addresses or
links contained in this book may have changed since publication and
may no longer be valid. The views expressed in this work are solely those
of the author and do not necessarily reflect the views of the publisher,
and the publisher hereby disclaims any responsibility for them.

The author of this book does not dispense medical advice or prescribe the use
of any technique as a form of treatment for physical, emotional, or medical
problems without the advice of a physician, either directly or indirectly. The
intent of the author is only to offer information of a general nature to help you
in your quest for emotional and spiritual well-being. In the event you use any
of the information in this book for yourself, which is your constitutional right,
the author and the publisher assume no responsibility for your actions.

Any people depicted in stock imagery provided by Thinkstock are models,
and such images are being used for illustrative purposes only.
Certain stock imagery © Thinkstock.

Print information available on the last page.

ISBN: 978-1-5043-5648-0 (sc)
ISBN: 978-1-5043-5649-7 (e)

Balboa Press rev. date: 09/21/2016

Dedicated to
Aslan, The Shy Huntress,
Susie, Mother
Little Love, The Odd Duck,
Pippi Chupacabra, The Unexpected,
Tredfoot, The Insatiable,
Tiberious the Tigger, Challenger of Fire,
Bandit, The Journey,

… and the Planet Earth,
which never fails to Inspire.

Grateful!

If you enjoy this little book,
feel free to give it to someone else to enjoy!

Dear Human Person,

Whether you are a little person of only a few years,
or a big person of many years, your life energy is
precious in this vast universe!
Every atom is accounted for,
you are known.

Once there was a tiny little pebble who didn't know
they mattered on such a vast rock as this earth,
inside this even more vast Universe.
One day a little bird picked up the pebble and
dropped him into a small glass of water.
The little pebble raised the water level just enough
that the little bird could finally get a sip of water.
The little bird looked at the pebble in gratitude.
Now, this little bird would have the strength to fly
back to her nest and care for her little chicks.

No matter what you do in your life,
it will affect all other life,
life you are aware of
and life you are unaware of.

Within you is a myriad of energized particles that
collaborate and celebrate in their way your very
existence.

You will likely never see them, or know them by name, but they make up you.

We hope you will choose well, be gracious, choose love, to be happy, kind to your little body, and embrace the whole that you are connected to.

As we all make this choice together and create the next moment.

-The Planet,
and me.

<u>About Find Your Happy!</u>
<u>and The Seven Observations:</u>

There are 7 amazing, little rocks, one rock comes from each of the seven continents that make up the Planet.

Together, they are called the Unity Rocks.

Each rock has an Observation they share, regarding some aspect of the human existence. They share how Nature has similar situations, and therefore, how it is handled within Nature.

This is Universal Wisdom, natural, divine, happy.

Their goal is to help close the gap between Humans and the Planet.

They want you to enjoy their little personalities, their sense of humor, and the Natural Wisdom inherent in us all.

This little book was written for anyone, any age with an affinity for rocks, nature, and creating good.

:)

We were born alive.

Born to live.

Not just exist,
to truly live.

I recommend doing it
out loud.

-Little Love

The Seven Observations Chapters:

Choose to Expand

-The Universe

The Seven Observations

1. The natural state of Atomic Coexistence found throughout the Universe in which all matter exists peacefully, happily.

2. Having the Universal Perspective, the power in focusing your attention, and choosing happiness.

3. Appreciation for Your Self creates a stronger, effective, powerful force for good, enables happiness.

4. Become Inseparable within your 'self'.

5. This Moment is the Fullness of Your Life. Stay within it, powerful, effective, and happy!

6. Feelings are meaningful ways the body communicates the truth of what is happening, allowing us opportunity to sincerely affect our well being, our happy.

7. Appreciating the value and enormous power of your words for creating good, moment by moment, for your 'self' and all others.

Begin now.

The First Observation
<u>Atomic Coexistence</u>

The natural state throughout the Universe in which all matter exists peacefully. Happily.

Hello. My name is Derek. I am of a Rock family called Basalt, found throughout the Planet. I am from a place called Asia, one of the seven continents.

My full name is Derek, The Gray Dream of Energy. I have the privilege of sharing the first of seven Observations.

Atomic coexistence is how all matter exists perfectly, harmoniously, happily, with respect and appreciation for the attributes of others. This is a natural state available at all levels of consciousness.
The Planet is at peace. Happy. My Observation is, however, that humans are not at peace. Not happy.

I know this matters. It's a critical issue for us all. When one component is out of whack, it matters.

My observation, and how I discuss it, may seem simplistic. I hope you will allow for this. It doesn't make the discussion less, it only keeps it simple.

It seems as though, for me to be effective, it may be necessary to let you know a little about me.

I am a rock.

I recently took on my first name,

Derek. This human tradition, using names, is unique, and fun! The 'surname' I have, is The Gray Dream of Energy. It is very meaningful to me.

I want to talk more about my family name, but first, let me explain just a dusting of what type of rock I am, since I found out I am a 'type'!

> *Atomic Coexistence is how all matter exists perfectly, harmoniously, happily.*
> *With respect and appreciation for the attributes of others.*

The human name for my type of rock is Basalt.

Over the time that humans have been present on the Earth, Basalt has been a rock used for many purposes. Humans often appreciate the healing type properties they associate with Basalt.

You may or may not agree with that possibility, that's fine.

I am appreciated for my heat, the power of fire.

Some even say I help with the flow of creativity!
I am an incredibly stable and a good friend for the
'tough' times.

Some say "A rock is a rock is a rock."
Meaning there is no difference, a rock is just that, a
rock.

There is truth to that.
The beauty of not differentiating, is that one is not
valued more than another. This is a natural, universal
truth. One rock is not more
'valuable' than another.

Atomic Coexistence is without judgement.

They might have different attributes
that are useful in different ways,
or appearances that are useful and
appreciated as well.

This is simply true.

Within the natural realm, one rock is equal to every
other rock. There are no class distinctions. Each
one is treated equally, all is fair. No separations or
judgements apply. This is critical to our peaceful
existence. We are truly united in this way, it is a
Universal Truth.

As a matter of fact, just to write this Observation, and be able to express myself, I had to learn what 'class distinctions', 'fair', and many other terms meant, since these do not exist in nature.

These are 'human specific' terms.

Atomic Coexistence involves appreciation for our various differences and attributes.

However…according to human ways, quite often things are given distinctions. One person or thing is made out to be more valuable than another based on these distinctions.

This is very relevant. It is not in line with natural wisdom, and as a result, noticeable disharmony results.

If the simple, little, rocks can be divvied up and one valued at crazy high money value, while another is valued at a money value of zero, what happens when that same type of valuation is applied to human life?

I know this is not a new thought. I will share more on how us rocks observe, communicate, and see human behaviors.

Right now I'm fired up! Excited. I often am.
I'm hoping that by letting you peek into my rock
world, we can become closer. If we can do that, well,
anything is possible!

The best way I can imagine doing this, is to explain
my surname, "Gray Dream of Energy". I'm not talking
about the type of rock I am anymore, but rather
an actual Dream… a Dream shared
throughout the Universe!
A Dream of Energy.
The Universe is full of surprises, just
like you and me.
So, don't be too surprised to learn that
the Universe even has a dream!

You have an amazing reality you may be unaware of.

This word 'dream' isn't being used like
the word 'dream' that you have when
you are asleep, and have a dream.
That is different.

The 'Dream' is a way of saying "our world" or "reality".
The Universe has a reality that all of Nature is
connected to.
Like when someone uses the phrase "living the
dream", they aren't saying they are living a fantasy.

Just an amazing reality!

The Universal Dream is an Amazing Reality!

The Dream of Energy. The 'Energy' part, is how you and I will connect and communicate. Just as nature all around is in constant contact, communication through it's energy interconnectivity. (Wow, that is a big word!)

Atomic Coexistence begins with a connection at the atomic level, an awareness to foster.

So you see, A Dream of Energy, is like living a very natural reality, being closer to nature, connected on many levels of awareness, and it's natural wisdom.

This is a tangible, feeling, place. It's not imaginary.
It is in your moment to moment existence.

Oddly enough, it's very different from what most humans look for and expect in the course of their reality. That's unfortunate, but part of why I wrote this! I want you to connect with nature, consciously, at the atomic level.
Knowingly. Purposefully.

Truth!

Now, I'm a rock, true.

I'm also all about Energy.

I've been connected to this planet, the Universe, everything, for a very long time. So, I know a little bit.

I'll start with something simple,... you call them "Atoms".

Don't fret, it's electrifying, hair raising, spine tingling... ok, maybe not, at least not for me, no spine, ha, and no hair!

Ok, Atoms, as you may know, are pretty much what everything is made up of. (Yes, you thought that you knew the ingredients in that cake recipe!)

At the atomic level you are in sync with your environment! No judgement, no prejudice. Perfect harmony between your self and every thing.

If we look at the atoms that make stuff up, we find that us rocks, well, we have much the same atoms that you humans have. Surprised? Like Carbon, Iron, water. We are more similar than you might imagine.

Take a moment, is your hand touching something?

Maybe a table? The tiny atoms that are on your skin, are whizzing around at a molecular speed of crazy, while the atoms on the table are doing that too.

No traffic lights, or turning lanes. No crashing. Just co-existing. At the atomic level you are in sync with your environment!

Put on your special atom locator glasses, (which ironically, are made out of atoms,) and Voila!

Every thing feels!

Now you can look around and see that everything you couldn't see moving, *is* moving. Incredibly fast too! (Yes, of course, we're pretending about the glasses. Unless you really do have a super cool pair! There are some nuclear physicists out there! Anyway, you can imagine it as good as it is!)

In the air all kinds of dust atoms, human stuff atoms, cat atoms, dog atoms, dinner atoms, clothing atoms, candle atoms, plastic atoms....

Non scientific terms thank you! I said I would keep it simple.
Simple it is.

Settled on the shelf are a myriad of atoms, they look so peaceful, but with your special atom glasses on you can see the activity!
Now, look at me, or really, any rock!

The atoms that make it up are whizzing around at breakneck, crazy, speed, yet, it looks so calm. Like me. I'm calm, yet excited. It's a wonderful combination.

Pick me up, your Unity Rock, or any rock, go on now, don't be shy. See with your minds eye, those tiny atoms, your skin, your atoms. Imagine what your atoms feel. Yes, feel.
Everything feels.

Time to say ...Hello!

Your atoms can feel the Rock atoms, they are aware, they co-exist, happily, whizzing around in their little zone.

At this level of awareness you are completely happy.
Feel everything.

This is a real aspect of your life, your existence. It's beautiful.

Close your eyes if it helps, think about a little tickle sensation.

Your fingertips start.
One awareness is the rocks texture. Now zoom in with the minds eye, see the atoms on the surface of the rock, feel a light tickle. Imagine it. Feel it!

The only thing to limit your feeling and seeing this is you. You already know it's real. Allow yourself to imagine. To feel this image.
You are touching energy! True.

You are energy!

It's a fantastic thing, your body made up of all kinds of whizzing super fast atoms. All these atoms are stuck together making the shape of you! With an amazing bond that keeps you intact, it's awesome!

Human made and the otherwise made exists perfectly, because there are no 'good' or 'bad' atoms.
Only respect and appreciation for the attributes of others.
This is Universal Wisdom.

The air against your skin are atoms with energy, and all these connecting with every single thing everywhere!

You are in contact with energy throughout the Universe! Truth.

Every thing has atoms, and you are connected to it all. Doesn't matter if it is human-made or otherwise-made. It all has atoms. All these atoms connect.

Nothing is alone. No thing is alone.

When you start feeling this energy, this is what we call Universal Energy. Mark my words, this is powerful juju! It's real.

Once you became aware of this energy, you connected. Some say it's like waking up to a dream where suddenly everything is ALIVE! Practice holding me, envision the atoms between you and me. Sometimes being in a quiet place helps.

Your awareness at this atomic level of your existence allows appreciation for all that is. In a world full of differences, there is this peaceful, wonderful, energy. Breathe. Feel. Happy.

Practice breathing in and out deeply. Breathing is very useful with helping you, as a human to feel stuff.

Soon you will have thoughts and feelings that will go from you to me.
Then, you will feel something coming back to you.
I am sharing with you.
Universal intelligence with a dash of humor!

Welcome to our dream human!
It's real :)

-Derek

There are endless reasons
to be unhappy.
It takes courage
to give them the finger,
figuratively, as I have no fingers,
and choose to be happy.

-*Tiberious and Aslan*

The Second Observation
<u>It's How You Look At It!</u>

Having the Universal Perspective, the power in focusing your attention, and choosing happiness.

Hello, My name is Starla. I am an Australian Citrine, the Zen of Happiness Rock from the continent of Australia. I'm here to talk about Happiness, as I am truly a happy, happy little rock!

My Observation with regard to human happiness, relates to perspective. You may think a little rock would have a little perspective. Not at all!

I am connected to this huge planet, as well as the rest of the Universe, so we share a gigantic, overall perspective. Having a nice perspective, is like a vantage point.

A bird, sitting on the edge of a cliff, looking over a canyon, seeing without any obstruction. Nice!

Then you add the power found in focusing your attention to the mix. Now the bird sees movement, perhaps prey in the grass, a mile away. Focus is the difference between an empty or a full tummy!

The bird makes choices, that lead to the end results. His power is in owning his choices. Creating the quality of the next moment.

Humans don't seem to know their power. I like to think my little Observation will encourage the connection each human has with their empowerment. Enhance perspective.

Discover the power in their focus, their attention.

Choose to own it.

Own choices, own happiness.

Is that heavy?

Wow, for a second it seemed kinda, but I choose powerful subject matter with a healthy dose of Sunshine and Happiness!

> 2. It's How You Look At It: Having the Universal Perspective, the power in focusing your attention, and choosing happiness.

Let me take a moment to tell you a bit about me, then I will get back to my Observation!

I can do serious, but always with humor. I am always ready to laugh, and smiling is the most wonderful amazing thing of all! Yes, I'm a rock, and yes, I smile.

I am in the Quartz family, a 'yellow' variety. (I learned

colors!) I am known to help clear away negative energy, and bring positive energy!

My color comes from a variety of minerals, I'm told, Ferric Hydroxide and maybe Aluminum also. I am from, and I represent the Continent of Australia. I am the Planet, as are you!

Breathe.
Feel.
Follow Your Breath!
This is your life.

-Tolle, Millman, Susie…
Paraphrased

I choose to represent Happiness. It suits me… I am also a bit blunt at times. No worries mate, you can handle it!

I have atoms in me that come from outer space. Seriously. That's why I was named Starla. A star fell to this planet ages ago, and some of its atoms are part of me. So, I can confirm to you that Universal energy, Universal Wisdom, (Universal Perspective!) it's big… Powerful, limitless, timeless, and supremely positive!

Let's start!
If possible, hold onto me, or any rock.
Take a moment to breathe in deeply.

Feel your tummy get bigger, your chest rise. Shoulders tall and straight. Take in as much air as you can!
Hold it while you read this next sentence.
No matter what age human or size human you are, this all works the same!

Now let out all that marvelous air...
Wait for a second, don't breathe yet.... notice, it's very quiet in this moment, smile big!
Now, take in your next breath.
Let your smile grow with the amount of air you breathe in!
They (your smile and the amount of air) are directly associated!

> "*The atoms are whizzing around at breakneck, crazy, speed, yet, it looks so calm.*
> *Like me.*
> *I'm calm, yet excited.*
> *It's a wonderful combination.*"
>
> -Derek

Do this often.
I love this, and it's good for you!
Which makes it good for all of us.
Ok, breathing and smiling, very important!

Energy.
Remember how Derek talked about Atoms, how every thing is made up of these little energized goobers?
How everything is connected?

All this coexistence in perfect harmony, no judgement, peaceful. This is positive.

To us, meaning, to all of nature, there is only one kind of energy, positive. (We don't even use the term 'positive' but we will use it now for clarity.)
No rock has ever had a negative idea, thought, or anything, it's just not natural.
We are pure positive energy.

> *Negativity does not exist in Nature.*

I want you to get just how overwhelmingly huge the positive energy is that abounds throughout everything, everywhere.
Consider the sun for this planet... now that is a lot of positive energy! Add to that the awesome power of all the stars, suns, planets and other stuff out there!

You are completely surrounded in a universe of positive!

If you can visualize how enormous it is, you'll understand how small the negative truly is, and this will provide Universal Perspective.
The point being, that most humans have been consumed by the negative, in their daily moment to moment.

The negative is so 'in your face' they don't see beyond it. That is having no perspective.

Without perspective their power, their attention, is on the only thing they see, the negative. It sits on the tip of the nose, so to speak!

It is a slow energy drain, moment by moment, day after day, year after year, it's miserable. We (us rocks) see humans in this situation, and it is unfathomable.
Take this moment, and try to visualize yourself.

No thing can create negative energy, only humans.
You are a very powerful creator.

Create wisely..

You are standing.

Hold out your hands in front of you, palms up.

In one hand you hold this *universal mass of positive energy.* Let's make it green, like a green basketball…

In your other hand, the *mass of human negative energy.* We can make it blue, or any color. It won't matter what color you pick, because you can't see it. It's too small.

Now the reason this is called 'human' negative energy, no insult intended, but just to be clear, the only negative energy that exists, is from humans. Nothing else can create it. Everything else is held to Universal Wisdom.

So, back to the comparison.

> *Whatever is getting your attention, becomes more and more powerful.*
>
> *Expanding or contracting your perspective.*

The hand holding the Positive Universal energy, is say, the size of a basketball. A giant, gelatinous, green, glowing, sphere of atoms.

You can peer into it and see the atoms whizzing around, it's cool, streaks of light, popping, vivid, exciting!
It looks totally bad ass awesome!
It's beautiful, powerful, mesmerizing. You might even find yourself smiling, it's fun, happy energy!

Your other hand, holding the mass of negative human energy, well, it looks like nothing is in your hand!
It's so infinitesimally small.
Yes, I'm talking about the MASS, the sum total of all human negativity that exists throughout all of time.

It's tiny, so small it is invisible to the human eye.

Ok, with so much positive energy out there, why does it seem like the bad is so monstrously huge, unfathomably evil, compared to the good? Why does the human condition seem permeated by so much bad energy? Why are so many, so unhappy?

Those are sincere, genuine questions, and I have an excellent answer. Bear with me now, I may use simple little examples, but it works!

Imagine for a moment that every week you go to a little corner store, and buy a pack of gum. Each time you go into the store, the same little clerk is behind the counter.

That bird I mentioned earlier, looking out over the canyon chooses to not be distracted by peripheral happenings. Empowering his self. He doesn't let his attention wander. The price is too high!

When you bring the gum up to the clerk, they look at the gum, turn it over, and look for the price, or the bar code, and each time they can't find it.

It doesn't matter that you have done this each week.

It's somewhat annoying, aggravating, insulting, infuriating...?
It is the perfect scenario for bad energy to thrive on.

You know before you go to the store, what is going to happen, and the negative self talk, begins. When you walk into the store, and see the same clerk, the negative energy grows. Now you get the gum, and you know what will happen next. Sure enough... it all plays out exactly as it did the last time.

Mechanical actions tend to be negative, and surprisingly unproductive.

They are Thought less.

You leave and go to work, school, wherever, and the negative energy is fostered as you go through your weekly routine. You relate this same happening with your friends, co-workers, class mates!

This little incident, along with the attention it was given, and then repeated, each week, is being fostered. (Although it is equally funny that your reactions are as repetitious as the clerks, creating the same result.)

This tiny little incident has become huge.

You aren't even paying attention to the gum you got!
That is just going on mechanically, chew, chew, chew.
While your mind repeats, replays, rehashes the incident.

You just spent a dollar of your hard earned money, to
chew gum you won't enjoy, because your brain is
rehashing an incident that has repeated itself every
week.

What made this little incident so
big that it consumed you before it
even happened, and now after the
fact is still consuming you?

The Attention it is given.

What gets attention is given power.
Or we could say, is empowered by
your attention.
Pause for a sec, it's true.

*It is
interesting to
think of
'thought' as
energy.
Just like a
'feeling' has
an energy.*

*It is your
energy to
create as
positive
or not.*

When something bad happens, it
gets announced, played over and over again, on the
news, at the water cooler, in the bathroom, over coffee...
Over and over again it is talked about.

Given attention.

The human mind empowers it, keeps it alive, expounds, expands, imagines scenarios, creates more and more, and all this 'thought' is energy... not the positive kind.

It is interesting to think of 'thought' as energy. It is a little different than the energy associated with an atom. Like a 'feeling' it has an energy. True, this is a 'different' kind of energy then particle energy. However, it is real, felt, even measurable.

Humans expose and rehash the negative. The idea of it and sometimes the reality of it gets more ugly. More and more powerful. All because of how much attention it is getting.

Your Attention is yours alone. You choose where to focus it. This is your power! Claim your power!

If your life were a game, are you on the bleachers watching it unfold? Hoping for an outcome, guessing what will happen, wishing? Drinking a soda and getting squishy?

Or, are you on the playing field, focussed on goals, passionate, making your own choices?

Either way, it is your life! You make the choice.

If you don't, others will take it, consciously or not.

From what I understand, just little me, a lot of research and money goes into taking human power and using it to control and direct other humans.

Try a little experiment.

Walk up to a small group of friends, co-workers, family, who are busily chatting away. Note to yourself, if their conversation is positive or negative.
You may find it is most often negative.
That's ok.
It helps explain this matter of how negativity abounds. Fostered by a lack of awareness, a lack of focus, the human condition of giving away their power!

A simple act, has great power.

Simple.
Action.
Owning.
Choosing.

Happy!

Another fun little experiment is to wait for a polite pause in the conversation, and bring up a new topic.
Something awesomely cool, positive, wonderful!
For instance, "Did anyone notice the beautiful Moon last night?"

You will likely find some small talk presents about the moon, then, often, sarcasm, or negativity returns.
It is an entrenched force. Like any habit, it requires conscious effort to move in a positive direction with thoughts, actions, reactions...

In the case of a simple trip to the corner store for a pack of gum, what choices can you make, to create a positive experience, knowing what you know?

> *Happiness is your choice.*
>
> *Get used to it!*

Be your own hero, change the entire experience into a positive force! When you leave for the store, you can smile knowing how silly it may all be. Entering the store, you can smile, engage the clerk, get their name, use it, change their day!
Hand the clerk the gum, smile, tell them the price, and you know how it's difficult to find.
Breathe, relax, enjoy the moment.
Connect with another human being if you possibly can! Your efforts create a meaningful reality.

Leave happy! Enjoy your gum, savor it, you chose it, you paid for it, give it a little attention!

These simple actions completely change the viewpoint. For yourself, and for the little clerk. Now it can even change anyone else that you relate it to.
Zero negative energy!
That is sweet!

Negative 'events' are everywhere in life. For some that is all they may ever see.
Everyone chooses.

Each human is powerful! Capable of taking action, eradicating the yuck. When you choose your focus, to be positive, you link into the powerful universal energy, and we all get stronger!
The more attention you give to positive things, the happier you will find yourself. The happier others around you will be also! It's a wonderful domino effect!

The universe is paying attention to all that is positive, you can too! Your new friend, me, is happy.
We all are. Sitting in our little space, happy, cozy. It's great.
How is it that we are happy? It's a choice.

I'm Happy and Cozy!

Let me show you a fun way that shows how being happy is a choice!

Take a moment, perhaps you can pick up a little rock, like me, connecting, breathing together, sharing energy. Wiggle your toes.

Now, you know the mechanics behind making yourself smile, so go ahead, put a big, juicy, smile on your little face!

Choose to be happy.

Create it with your power of choice.

Focus your attention wisely.

Laugh at the tiny negative, and be part of the positive!

I know it's 'forced', that's ok.

Just do it, this will be fun! Can you see yourself? In a mirror, or in your minds eye? It's kinda funny how a fake smile looks.

Now make it even bigger, widen your eyes, raise your eyebrows, show those teeth, suck in more air!

Hold it!

Keep holding it! 30 seconds.... do your cheeks hurt? Longer! 60 seconds!

Now you feel silly and your smile has become real! You created your own happy moment! Happiness, it was a choice!

Do this little exercise any time you want, but especially when some negative is happening and you need to shake it! (Including the negative stuff that routinely may creep into your thoughts!)

You get to choose the positive!
Notice how peaceful it feels. A nice energy. Others will notice if you smile more, that's a good thing! You are helping to create more positive energy!

Next time something negative starts looking monstrous, instead of being afraid, stressing out, cracking up... choose your focus, give the situation true perspective. Create your choices, honor them with actions, and this is all positive!
If nothing else, think of something beautiful, happy, peaceful. Redirecting your attention, giving your power to something of your choice!

Smile. It's good.
That's a positive action taken.

-Starla

Challenge your 'self'…

Take an every day event
and turn it into a
fun, meaningful,
every day positive!

You have such power.

-Starla and Tredfoot

The Third Observation
<u>Atomic Chow and Pet Juju</u>

Appreciation for Your Self creates a stronger, effective, powerful force for good, enabling happiness.

Hi. My name is Brian, and yes, I too am a Unity Rock. My Observation is on the relationship between your human self and food. How this relationship is crucial to human self empowerment, and thereby your being happy!

I include 'pets' in my Observation, because they are so much a part of the human day to day happiness, and we all love food!

As I said I am a Rock. I'm the European Jade Bomb, Agate with Gratitude dude. Yes, I do think I'm funny, I crack myself up all the time, so don't try to burst my bubble!

I love my green! (I love Kermit!)

I love food!

I love animals!

I love funny!

If I were an adult human, you might thing I was a little immature. Really, I'm simply a happy rock.

That is not the same as being 'stoned!" lol. Rock humor!

I love to hit the food topic. If you ever want to give a rock a snack, try fruity pebbles, or rock salt on cucumber. Haha!

Your experience with sensations and feelings, are shared with us. Every thing around you is shared positive energy.

Us rocks, we feel everything. That is truth. Now that you are connected with Derek, Starla, and me, what you feel, we feel!

As you know, feelings are transmitted by energy, wonderful, positive, energy!

As rocks we understand how humans must eat. You eat food and drink water or you will cease to exist as a human.

First let me explain how the food experience you have is connected to me, and then I'll explain how us rocks eat, and how that is connected to you!

We enjoy and appreciate the food you experience if you try this one thing...

Slow down when you eat!

You can experience the sensations of hot, cold, texture, sweet, sour, bitter, tangy. To do so fully, takes a little bit of time. So... breathe.

> *Slow down, breathe!*

Breathe during and in between bites.

Sounds obvious, but with all the air around, you would think there was a shortage! It seems y'all don't ever truly get enough!

Seriously now, take a moment in between bites and simply breathe. Feel what your body is experiencing, truly listen.

> *Being able to share this experience with your entire body creates a strong connection within you. A crucial step in self empowerment.*

Appreciate the tastes, sensations, and feelings. Let your entire body have the moment to enjoy each bite! Most often humans eat, and only taste with their mouth, feeling full after a bit, in their tummy.

It takes practice and time to share the experience, with your entire body.
Even your toes have an opinion!

45

Being able to share this experience with your entire body creates a strong connection within you. This is also considered 'self awareness'.

This connection can grow, given a little attention. Remember, we talked about how powerful your attention actually is! You create and promote internal communication.

"Appreciation for your self makes you powerful!

A stronger force for good on the planet."

-Brian

Yes, you could call it 'talking to your self'.

This is good, positive energy!

First it's about slowing yourself down, and breathing. Next, chew each bite meaningfully. Don't underestimate the value of each chew, each breath. Notice what your body is feeling as you eat.

Think about each cell in your body getting nutrition from the bite in your mouth. Each atom skipping around refreshed! Feel the appreciation your body has for you taking care of it. It needs you.

When you get really good at this 'feeling your body has' you will connect with every part of your body and be able to communicate together!

Angel talks about this more in Chapter 4.

Tell yourself, "This bite of food is truly significant", then, "I love each and every one of you little cells, and atoms, and this food is me taking care of you!"

If you can, visualize your cells, your atoms, getting oxygen, getting nutrients, and smiling at you, your body appreciates your attention.

If that is hard to visualize, imagine your body is like a small child, looking up at you as they munch on a yummy piece of watermelon, happily. Eyes bright and shiny, glowing with appreciation!

Paying attention to how your body feels will never be a waste of time. This is your soul mate!

If you focus your attention on each bite, each chew, each sip, each breath, your body will literally feel the love you are supplying it.

It kinda smiles back at you with feeling!

This might sound kinda funny, but it really works! Your body literally thrives under this kind of connection! More nutrients are absorbed, health benefits of all kinds are related to this kind of relationship with food.

Your body is your best friend. Truth.

Your body is the only friend you will ever have who is completely faithful and true to you in every way. Does what you say, goes where you say, it has a loyalty to you that goes beyond the mind.

With you every day, every breath until the day your breathe goes out, and doesn't return.

Imagine a bird, or a cat, as they groom themselves. They seem to do it for a very long, long time. Why? It's part of the natural relationship all of us have with our selves.

Every little cell in your body has gratitude for being nurtured.

Taking care of self by lovingly providing nutrition, caring, and taking the time to appreciate your little self.

Thank you for taking the time!

The attention. It's valuable.
We respect that. What you are experiencing creates feelings, thoughts, hence energy, and we are connected! So we get to experience it too! It's wonderful.

Just like you can watch a duck in a pond, swim around, dive, and catch a little minnow, gulp it down happily. You enjoy watching that duck. It's fun! In this case, you are like the duck, and us rocks, we are happily observing you!

Taking care of your self creates a stronger positive force for good! That is powerful truth. Imagine if every 'one' took care of themselves, how powerful the collective energy would be!

We would be unstoppable! We already are!

Every one, and every thing, are nourished by energy in some form.

Now I said I would explain a little about how us rocks 'eat'. Do us Stoners eat food? No. Not exactly. The truth is, that everyone and every thing are nourished by energy.
We all are 'nourished' at the atomic level.

"A rock may appear inert, inanimate. However, no thing exists without purpose. Including me."

-Brian, the rock.

Here is an example, a cat and a tree.

They both can eat a mouse. Yes, they can. Just let me explain. They eat very differently.. I don't think we will ever see a tree catch a mouse. Yet, a tree can eat a mouse. Very differently then the cat. The tree would absorb the nutrients out of the soil that the mouse is buried in. It would take time.

Funny thing is, if that were an apple tree, then the tree absorbs the mouse nutrients, sucks them up and makes apples. Then a human comes around, takes an apple, eats it. Are you eating a mouse or an apple? Haha! This is another great example of how we are all connected.

> *Happiness is far deeper than any action, circumstance, or thing.*

Not to be freaky, but if a human dies, and gets buried, and a tree grows, same scenario, you eat the apple, are you a cannibal?

The idea that a rock can eat, is simply the same as saying a tree eats. It is not what you might eat, or the way you would eat, but it is the same essential process.

Sometimes we don't understand something, but that doesn't mean that it isn't happening.

Now, I like to mention a little bit on how my Observation relates to your 'pets'. Many humans have amazing relationships with animals, and this is a huge positive!

Tell me again about "Atoms"?

Okay, then you tell me about "doodoo"?

It might be just as important as food and water for you! It creates wonderful, positive energy that the entire plant benefits from and loves!

Thank you! Every tiny effort towards kindness, love, and caring for others, animal, human, planet, or rock, is part of your being happy.

Happiness is your choice. Even when you are out cleaning up dog poop.

Maybe you aren't euphoric, at that moment. However, your happiness is far deeper than that action, or circumstance.

You can hum a little tune, and throw the ball while you clean up dog poop. That's a great, happy choice.

No 'thing', no 'one', can 'make' you happy. Not even a puppy! It is the choice you made to get the puppy, to care for it, to love it, that creates your happiness! The puppy is frosting!

When you view happiness as something you create, and own, it removes all the things that get used as excuses for being unhappy.

You no longer have things that "make you" unhappy. Because no thing can 'make' you unhappy. Only you can.

If you didn't clean up the dog poop for a week, so now it's a mountain of a job, it isn't the dog poop making you unhappy. It is the choice you made not to do it, and the resulting circumstances.

Similarly, no thing would 'make' you happy.

Again, you are the creator, only you can create, by where you focus your attention. Creating positive goodness, or not. You make choices, each choice has a result. Create positive. Make conscious, meaningful choices. About food, how you eat, breathe, play, …

Let your choices empower you! You become stronger with each choice!

Just like when you choose to love on your pets, the happier we all are! The fuzzy, furry, fluffy, soft wonderfulness. The lick factor, the nose kisses, the nuzzling. We love hearing your lovey sounds. Talk about happy atoms! Powerful juju happening with pets!

You take a bath with your tongue, Wow, why not water?

Kittys Water

It licks me back!

Positive energy grows at a fantastic rate when humans, animals and all of nature get along. It's unbelievably powerful good energy!

We all share the same atoms.

The more you can see the similarities among us all, the differences fade, we become unified, and this creates more and more positive energy! Your home grows exponentially into the Universe! Focus your attention on all that we share in common, appreciate the value of food, breath, loving, touching, nurturing, bathing, grooming, giving.

> *Your home grows exponentially into the Universe!*

Feel any separation fade.
Feel any division fade away.
Choose this.
This is a powerful thing! Imagine if the entire planet of humans were to let all the things that cause separation go away....
Be grateful, happy, show your appreciation, show your love, the energy around you will become more powerful!

This is wonderful!   *-Brian*

The PBJ Affirmation

"Thank you grape jelly.
Thank you yummy peanut butter.
Thank you soft bread, melting in my happy mouth.
My little cells are smiling and know this food is
specially for them!"

Every thing feels love.
Love every thing.

-Brian, me.

The Fourth Observation
<u>The 3 Amigos</u>

Become Inseparable within your 'self'.

Does it seem odd to you that I am a rock, and you are reading my 'words'? This is perhaps the easiest form of communication for a rock to enjoy, as being 'heard' is not so easy!
My name is Angel, I have the fourth Observation to share, and I am a black Onyx rock.

I'm pleased to say, my family name is The South American Black Onyx, with Love. My Observation simply stated, is "Become Inseparable within your 'self'."

There are seven of us Unity Rocks, you have met three before me. Derek, Starla, and Brian. We are each from a land mass on this planet, you call Continents. We are inseparable, joined by the planet!

We are called Unity Rocks because we are unified within our selves, and with each other!
By contrast, I have observed, that humans are divided, both within their individual self, and as a whole. This is not natures way, and it does not create happiness!

The Universe sets the example of how being Inseparable is best for the individual and as a result, best for the whole. I'll definitely talk more about that! However, being inseparable is very much about Love.

Yes, I'm talking about the 'L' word! Each individual must 'choose to choose' love for their 'self'. That sounds kinda funny, but it's true!

Being Inseparable is best for the individual and as a result, best for the whole.

Being Inseparable is Loving.

Apparently I'm a good one to bring this topic to the fore, you see, Black Onyx is a rock associated with protection, which is a form of love in action.

This is the protection of 'self'. You have to protect your self from various energy drains in life situations. Energy drains are when you are being divided by all kinds of things sneaking in and subtly, or not so subtly, stealing your energy. Diverting your focus.

Protecting your 'self' to promote healing, to remain or get grounded, to ensure your best possible stability.

One can protect themselves by increasing their stamina and endurance or by using self control. Not allowing some destructive temptation to thwart your 'self'.

Hanging out with me, appreciating our energy, could be a powerful way to connect within your 'self'. I can be a little reminder towards putting *your* love towards *your* 'self' into action!

Sometimes humans lump stuff together under an umbrella, and call it "loving themselves". I prefer to be a bit more specific.
That's the way I am, and I'm pretty solid on that!

Loving your 'self' can be more real to you.

It's not a selfish, negative thing.

It is Loving.

In case you find it distracting that I use the word 'yourself' as your 'self', there is a reason for it! I am trying to emphasize that you, in essence, are the proud owner of your 'self'.

I mention this because I want to talk about the internal division humans have a great deal of, and part of that conversation involves the relationship you have with your 'self'.

57

It is a funny human thing where the brain and the body seem to have their own thoughts. When they communicate, listen to, care for, and respect the other, this is an inseparable bond that empowers the whole 'self'.

That awareness is very important in all these Observations, which often point towards you making choices.

The best choices are made when you take as much into consideration as possible, between you and 'self'.

> *It may seem so simple, it can be mistaken for unimportant*
>
> *There is no such thing as unimportant*

For instance, you are aware you need to go to the bathroom. You know because your body tells you. That is communication within your 'self'. You in turn, respond, listen, and go take care of business.

That is love, protection of your 'self' by caring for you. Simply put, you feel better, happy!

That is a nice, pleasant internal conversation, with a happy ending. It's a great example of unity, or what I call being inseparable.

While us rocks are a great example of unity, being inseparable, there is another example, one I think you may find curious.

I'm going to talk more now about Love. I'm going to show you a crazy, awesome example it is of being inseparable, and how it relates to the universal wisdom of being happy!

Love is discussed so many ways, and often as though it were some sort of accident, you 'fall' into it, you are born into it, it just 'happens'… as though you have no power of choice with this mysterious, powerful force. Sound familiar? Kinda like *Twilight Zone* stuff. Hmmmm….

> *Universal love is like the atmosphere, the air around you, it is ever present*

That's not where we're going with this.

The love I'm talking about is Universal Love. The love that abounds throughout all of nature, the unconditional love that simply is. This love is like the atmosphere. Love is ever present.

Just like the air around you, sometimes when something

is so abundant, it is not seen at all. Seen or appreciated, even when it is crucial to sustain life!

Notice that when you take a breath, you have all the air you could want and more. How nice is that! Yet, so easy to take for granted.

Now, imagine that breath is love. You can take it in, all you could ever want, simply breathing it in. Love is that present around you.

Love actually is in the air!

Like Anchovies, Oxygen, warmth from the Sun... There is no shortage on the planet of love. Why? Because love is part of Universal Wisdom, it just makes perfect sense. Choose to notice, to see it. Observe love all around you, especially in nature.

> *Choose to notice! Observe love is happening and simply is all around you.*
>
> *Inseparable throughout all of nature.*

As reliable as the apple falling to the ground because of gravity, or knowing the exact time the sun will rise on any given day. Love is ever present, abundant, inseparable in all of nature.

When you choose to notice, you will see the love all

around, you can make the next step in this Observation quite easily. You see, love is inseparable with two other things. Happiness and Gratitude. Once you become aware of this reality, your own inseparableness gains momentum!

There is great universal wisdom in this little trio. They form such a perfect connection and energy, that when you feel one, the other two are always present. Always.

Love, Happiness, and Gratitude, I call them the Three Amigos! Let me show you how they work.

Imagine you are walking barefoot, and you step on a thorn, or a lego, or a tack! You're hopping around, thinking and saying any number of colorful things.

Love, Happiness, Gratitude.

The Three Amigos.

Finally you get brave, sit down, and look at the damage. Relieved there is no gushing blood! It has to come out. So, deep breathe, you pull it out. Yay! A fleeting moment of *Gratitude* that it came out without a hitch, whew! You immediately feel better, a little *Happiness* creeping in! Don't you just *Love* it when things work out!

It's not a trick. This moment really does have all three components. It is a cascade type of effect.

Now, you challenge yourself, and take any moment that you feel one of the Three Amigos, and walk yourself through it, find the other two!

They are always there! They refuse to be divided. Even in minute, trace amounts, they are there!

> *Your power is within you, inseparable.*
>
> *There is no other place for it to be.*

Practice this, turn it into a game. The more you play, the more you will find it's true. It takes only choosing to find the positive. Choosing to want it. This trio, they coexist perfectly. A perfect demonstration of unity. When you feel love, happiness, and gratitude, you are connected to powerful energy! It feels amazing!

Remember how I said Love was everywhere, in everything, as abundant as the air you breathe? Well, guess what! That means Happiness and Gratitude are also, they just have to be noticed, looked for, found.

Appreciating the unity, the inseparable nature of Love,

Happiness, and Gratitude as stepping stones toward your own empowerment. Your being inseparable.

As I have stated, my Observation is that humans are divided, both within their individual self, and as a whole.

This is not natures way.

Let me show you a brief description of the division we can observe in 'humankind'.

First of all humankind divvied up the planet. Yes, the seven land masses, continents, all given names. Then within the continents, all kinds of nations. Within the nations, cities. Within the cities, communities, neighborhoods, schools, teams... Of course within each of these there are always the ones who believe they are the 'superior' and the 'others' are the lesser.

*Choosing to choose.
Many opportunities for choice come and go unnoticed, unchallenged.*

Own Yours!

So now that everyone is divided up geographically, more divisions happen. I'm sure you can imagine. Socio economic, athletic prowess, skin color, beliefs, gender...

Of course within each group are more sub-groups. Always a winner, always a loser, always someone faster, someone slower, someone right, someone wrong....

Finally, and most importantly, you are each divided within your self. If you have straight hair, you want curly. If you have blue eyes, for some reason, you want brown. Have small boobs, want bigger boobs,.... uh huh.

> *Make a choice.*
> *Decide to stop your personal division within your 'self".*
>
> *This is loving.*

If it's not a physical division, it's emotional. You divide within yourself, get angry at yourself, feel guilt, regret, shame, discontent, jealousy.

Instead of being rock solid, you are divided, held together by the sheer benefit of atmospheric pressure! You are the only species that will beat yourself up all day because you woke up late this morning!

This is division. You have been divided, and conquered. Oddly enough, by yourselves.
A bird does not do that.
A jaguar does not.

Nor does a rock, a tree, or even a dust bunny!
The rest of the planet, the entire universe is in harmony
with itself, unified, inseparable.
Only humankind has diverted.
Has divided itself.

Division creates weakness, a lack
of power. It devastates happiness.
However, this division is not a
requirement, you can choose
otherwise.

What are your choices? Within this
moment, you can choose simply to
look for other choices, to not accept
what may be, simply because it is
the 'norm'. Stopping the division
is done moment by moment, in each individuals life.
Even milli-second by milli second!

Loving your 'self' will be an action.

Stop.

Breathe.

Tell your 'self' "I'm here. I am inseparable."

Most important will be stopping the division within
your little 'self' first. You must actively love your 'self'
and become inseparable. This is why I talked about
internal communication earlier. For you to become
inseparable, not divided within, it is imperative that
you choose to listen and love your 'self'.

How?

Take a moment, breathe it in.
Breathe in the air, the love surrounding you. Be grateful, happy. Choose this.

Breathe it in, and out.

Loving your 'self' sets you against the mainstream of human behavior, so it takes vigilant effort!

If it was the norm, the planet would be a very different place!

Let's create that!

Now, THE unifying force, within you, will be Loving your 'self'. You can achieve that by paying attention to your 'self'. Listen to the gentle signals your body is sending.

This can take a surprising amount of consistent effort! Don't get discouraged. You are basically setting yourself against the flow of mainstream human thought processes, and re-formatting your little brain body! That is HUGE in concept alone. In reality, it will get easier over time.

Start by noticing what your thoughts are doing. For instance, say you are invited to a party. That should be a good thing, fun, exciting! Perhaps that is your initial feeling.

Now notice that you had a moment of being unhappy with your 'self' because you gained some weight, and won't look the way you want to look for this party. Perhaps your favorite jeans don't fit.

That is DIVISION. Pay attention, it's trying to creep in! In that second you sent negativity to your body, to your thighs.
Notice this happening. Don't disregard it as not being meaningful. The only way to get your thighs to be what you want will be a series of cooperative actions with you and your 'self'. So, communicate lovingly, quit beating your 'self' up!

Breathe deep. Tell your 'self' "I love you, it's ok."

Smile for you. Comfort you. Be there for you.

Challenge where that thought came from! Perhaps it is a socialized concept of perfect thighs, and it may not be realistic for your body type.

Don't accept a social concept of perfection as yours, unless you consciously choose that to be yours.

You must find your inseparableness. Your little thighs are the only ones you will ever have.

They will take you anywhere and everywhere, just work with them. You are a team.

This is the time to find your happy!

All of this dialogue happens in a fraction of a second.

Notice that instead of happily planning to go to a party, division dumped a load of crap on your party!

> *Find your happy!*
>
> *Say to your 'self', "Ok, where is my happy? We can do this!"*
> *Take the time.*

Choose your happy! That is what some humans call this moment. It is a time when you say to your 'self', "I want my happy". It is like a trigger to help you return to the happy moment you were just at. It works really well once you get into the practice of it.

You will find that division happens constantly at first.

Now you are at the party, let's say. Notice that your mind flits around, you think "That boys cute, oh but wait, he would never like me." or "I should have shaved my legs, crap!". Then "My gift isn't that great, maybe I should just quietly slip out." and "I didn't feed Felix before I left, darn it, what an idiot." "Tomorrow I need to get gas, why didn't I do that already!"

This is DIVISION.

Think about this for a second. You went to all
the effort to go to this party and you aren't even
enjoying yourself because you are so divided by all of
yesterdays, todays, and tomorrows stuff.

Find your happy.
Focus.
Breathe.
Trust.
Find the Gratitude.
Find the Love! Love your 'self'!
Yesterdays often are dwelt on so
with guilt or remorse. It's over,
live and learn. Right now, enjoy
this moment. This is the moment
you are living in. Make it precious!
Choose to love on your 'self'!
Tomorrow can create anxiety, it isn't here yet, plan,
be constructive. Living is happening right now. The
choices within this moment, are right now!

> *"I Choose to completely, without any exceptions, no matter what, love me as me.*
>
> *This moment is mine."*
>
> *-Me*

Remember when Starla talked about where you
focus your attention, that is what gets your energy, it
matters! This is your moment, your energy, your life!

If you put your attention (your power) on things you don't like those things will get stronger, basically sucking the life, potential, and enjoyment out of you.

Creating division within you.
When you are divided, you are weakened, less powerful, less effective. You doubt your choices, decisions, everything becomes more complicated, less fun, weighty.

Your quality of each moment is compromised.

Each time you think something or see something about yourself you don't like, get fired up!
Challenge it!
Why do you think its not ok? Why are your thighs not perfect? Who or What says?

Be Truly Brave!

Don't cave.

Challenge and direct your thoughts.

Be inseparable, powerful.

Be truly brave. Love your little 'self'!
Choose to find your happy! . Choose to be unique, to be you, and completely accept yourself. As you are. Now. In this exact moment! Be inseparable! Be like a rock!
The universe will agree with you and will make you stronger.

Humans that choose to do this, and it takes effort, especially at first, truly stop seeing the negative things. Can you imagine not 'seeing' chubby thighs? What a relief!

Benefit from the full force of universal power as it removes obstacles in your thoughts. Only positive, loving, confident, happy, solution oriented thoughts happen.

It's very healthy, it's fun, peaceful, and feels amazing. Just refocus when a negative tries to wriggle in. It happens.

As you sharpen your awareness, you become more aware of your thoughts, and deciding how you want to think.

You will claim your power.

Take that moment, empower yourself, choose what you will think, don't cave, don't be led. You choose.

Here is another example of internal division. Let's say for example you decided to go for a nice walk in the evening after your dinner, or do your homework. Now suddenly you feel lazy and are waffling. So easy to just blob over to the couch and watch the boob tube!

This is division.

Remember, you already made this decision.

Don't rethink it. You made a great decision.

Has anything changed that requires you to rethink it?
Like a hurricane? No? Then stick to your decision, feel
good about it, and grow stronger!

This is loving! Protecting your decisions, backing
them up with active choices!
Each time you do this you create
momentum, it gets easier!

*Negatives
wriggle in,
that's ok,
refocus.*

*Trust your
'self'.*

*Regroup
often.*

Seems overly simple, yet it is
powerful truth. Encouraging 'self'
Love, Happiness in your choice,
and Gratitude that you did it!

Each individual can empower
themselves, become inseparable.
Thus stopping any negative
creepers from gaining momentum in your world, your
dream, the one you share with the Universe, with us!

When you choose the positive, you create a positive self
environment that others will be drawn to! It's amazing!
(Have you noticed how humans are drawn to rocks, that's

kinda why!)

Be the person that you would be drawn to because of their happy, loving, gracious disposition. Loving yourself with complete acceptance is felt by others, it's warm, wonderful, nurturing, exciting, sexy, crazy, happy,... You have an entire universal community full of positive energy to hang out with, and we are good company!

There is a funny human phrase, 'misery loves company'. Misery loves any company! Contributing only negative. Empowering it, and thus perpetuating more to be created. When you find yourself in or around this type of environment, try to get away, or if you can change the topic, anything to make the positive energy your focus!

Loving your 'self' feels wonderful, exciting, crazy, sexy, fun, happy!

You are good company, in good company!

The planet is in universal harmony. Now you are just like a tiny flower that begins to grow. It doesn't worry about water, sun, or anything. It gets stepped on, it just shrugs it off, and recovers. No blaming, just taking care of itself, it grows. Returning to its happy!

No gossip, grief over losing a petal, or not being as tall as another. The flower has its attention on the moment it is in.

Being wonderful. Growing. Even when that flower will succumb to death, it will do so without reservation. No fear, anxiety, grief, regret.

You are a perfect little flower.

Happy. Alive.

Inseparable within our shared existence.

Now that is a peaceful loving existence. Looking upon that tiny little flower is peaceful.

Feels nice.

This is connecting to the natural, positive energy. It's great. This is not an over simplification on life. You'll see.

The unity, the inseparable nature of the universe, and the inseparable attributes in the air you breathe, and all around you of Love, Gratitude, and Happiness are here to empower your efforts. We support you!

-Angel

Reclaiming My Moment:

"This is my time.

This is *my* time.

My moment.

My happy is here.

It's ok. I can give this to me.

I love all of me, as I am in this moment."

-Me

The Fifth Observation
<u>This Magic Moment</u>

This Moment is the Fullness of Your Life, stay within it, powerful, effective, and Happy!

Hi. My name is Darling, and I am a darling! I love the warm, fuzzy feeling that humans have when I meet them, and they call me 'Darling!'. A word can mean so much, it's amazing!

My Observation is about time, a powerful word! You see, this moment we are sharing right now, means a lot to me. It is the only moment that exists. My entire life is right now, about meeting you and telling you these words.

A moment ago… is gone.
A moment from now, nope, not here yet.
This moment is the fullness of life. Yours. Mine.

The key is staying within the moment.
Appreciating and living it to the full!
Have you ever heard the phrase "You only live once!"?
Well, you only live this moment once. Appreciating this moment, its value, its reality, is supremely powerful.

This is part of being truly happy and empowering your 'self'!
My Observation is very important because all of Nature lives within the moment.
You can call this the Universal Time zone.
Humans however, tend to live in multiple time zones.
I'll get into what I mean and why it matters!

I'm not a big talker, so this will be short and sweet! Like me! As you know, I'm a rock, I'm one of the Antarctic White Now. My stone is White Marble.

I have little facets to me that make me sparkle a bit, I'm usually all white in appearance. Sparkley!

We only live this moment.

Without this moment, there is no thing.

My Observation is about Time. It's about time that it be discussed, and it is about Time. Hehe!

So, white now, oops, I mean, right now, (haha), I'm going to start by relaxing. Let's do that. Just breathe in and out naturally, feel your body getting oxygen, love, energy!
Know that all of us connected to you appreciate you taking this moment!
Taking this time.

Universal Time is best explained as the only time that exists. It is the only time the universe, all the planets, all of nature use. It is also easy to refer to it as 'this moment'.

The kind of time that humans use is often referred to as 'clock time'. Humans have created 'clock time' from all of the events throughout the universe which run in natural cycles.

Universal time can be summed up as 'This Moment' also the 'Only Moment'.

The universe doesn't plan it, or do according to a schedule, they are the schedule. They just do. Notice that the universe never runs out of time, or over time. Is never late, or early.

It happens to be quite convenient that what they do is cyclic, and allows 'clock time' to exist. A convenient method humans use constantly and reliably.

It's interesting to note that what may appear to be the universe, or planets, suns, stars, moons, all moving in space without any seeming purpose, ends up providing a system, 'clock time' that humans use and rely on for most every thing.

For instance humans know when the sun will rise, using clock time. A bird also knows when the sun will rise, by perhaps instinct, or universal time.

The difference can be that a human sets the alarm, and wakes up, hits the snooze button, figuring they will adjust. Just ten more minutes before 'dealing' with the day.

By contrast, the bird will embrace that first glimmer of a new day, there is no snooze button! Up and doing, within that moment what needs to be done to ensure his well being and survival.

It's not an oppressive action. It is a productive, appreciative action.

It is living that moment.

Truly appreciating this moment will ensure quality, happiness, and productivity.

This is simply a difference, a gap between the human concept of time, and the potential use of universal time. My goal is to show how closing that gap will benefit you, creating a powerful, effective, and happy reality!

Time is a funny thing. Right now is a particular time, right? Let's say it's 2:00 O'Clock.

It's also called "Right Now".

Right now, you and I are new to each other. In time, perhaps next week, you might be exactly where you

are right now, and it will be that time again, you know, "Right Now".

It will still be 'right now' but a week later! I think that is amusing! Time is an interesting subject.

'Right Now' is 'Now'. You may find others use terms like "being in the now" or "in the moment". Also, being "present" or just "being". I like our term, I think Starla may have mentioned, about finding your "happy" within this moment, now.

Clock time is a useful tool, to use as needed to function in life events.

Universal time is your life.

Us rocks, we don't know "Time" as it is on a clock. That is a distinctively human concept. We adapt somewhat to use clock time so that we can communicate more easily with you. However, what we do know, is Now. We are always within the moment. Now. So is the rest of the universe. So are you, as this is the only moment you can directly affect.

You know this to be true, but I'll elaborate.

Humans tend to live in multiple time zones. The Past, Present, and Future.

The Universe, lives in one. The Present. As a result, each moment is used fully. Not diluted by the others. Nothing is ever wasted, not even one moment. Why does it matter?
A moment ago... is gone.
A moment from now, nope, not here yet.
This moment is the fullness of life.

In nature each moment is used to the full.

No-thing is wasted.

The moment is the fullness of life.

You cannot be at your most powerful, effective, happiest if you are not living in the moment. It's like being two places at the same time, one foot in the present, and one in the past or future. It's not effective.

Your attention diluted has less quality.

Only the present moment is in effect.
The past is over, done, finished. Learn from and move on kinda deal. You can identify when you have a foot in the past because it often has regret, guilt, remorse,

depression associated with it. If you are feeling things like that, pay attention, you are likely not living this moment as best you can!

The future isn't real yet. You can plan, but don't obsess. If you have a foot in the future, often it's evident by feelings of anxiety, 'what if', the unknown.

Your feelings will tell you if this moment is being diluted by the past, or the future.

Again, you can notice what you are feeling, identify it, and appreciate that you can affect the future moment much more powerfully by putting your all into this moment! What you do Now, will either benefit or not, the next moment.

I mentioned I am White Marble. I'm the perfect rock for this conversation as I am often associated with Power and Perseverance. Qualities that assist in calming anxiety and relieving depression.

Perhaps if you think of my sparkly, white, darling little self, you can use me as a reminder to identify what you're feeling.

Notice what you are feeling! When you recognize that you are dwelling on the past, something you cannot change, you can actively adjust so the mistake is not repeated.

Perhaps you are anxious, not prepared for something that is happening the next day, or in an hour?

Being present, coming back to your happy, would be asking yourself "What can I do, right now, in this moment that would make me happy?"

Often there is something, no matter how small, that can help relieve the anxiety and prepare you for what's coming.

Make a note, hang it on the mirror, or the fridge, read it out loud,

"What can I do right now to help make me happy?"

This is huge! It is putting your 'self' into action. It is being decisive. It is powerful!

Remember how powerful your attention is when it is focused? Choose to focus. This moment is the fullness of your life in many very true ways. Your attention and the quality you put toward this moment affects every future moment.

Right now is of absolute prime importance.

Ever notice how much you appreciate it when someone gives you their full attention? Try to be that person. Each interaction you have with another, give it your fullest attention.

Notice the immediate benefit.
The appreciation you will have and feel from whomever you are talking to will present. Maybe not immediately, but over time.

> *The value of each interaction you have is affected by the quality of your attention.*

The quality of your interaction, you'll feel. You'll remember more, the experience will hold more value.

The saying "Quality over Quantity" has validity in this sense. Sometimes you only get a few moments with another. With Quality, those moments are precious. It takes choosing to give your attention to the moment. To live it, and share it with another. This is a precious gift to your 'self' and to others!

When you live this way, on universal time, there is no room in the moment for anxiety,(because that would imply you were thinking about the future, or past) No space for guilt, remorse, or anything yucky.

If you are truly focused on reading these words, you cannot be feeling bad about loosing your temper yesterday. You won't be anxious about paying the rent next week. Give yourself that quality in each moment.

Practice on your 'self'!
By giving each moment your attention you will be highly productive, effective, you'll have your happy!

Observe how beautifully productive nature is, living to the full in each moment, no distractions.

You may notice how when humans are in the past or the future, it slows everything down. Like they are frozen, or moving through deep snow.

They just rehash past issues, or the upcoming future issues, over and over, *it ceases all productivity,* all quality is lost, love is squashed. It's not happy. When you notice this, it will help you to avoid doing it yourself.

Let me share an example, an amazing creature on this planet, the Falcon.

The Falcon that flies high above the earth, drifting on warm air that rises, and lifts him up. He searches, seemingly with no effort at all, for his next meal. His instinct and skills he has been developing from birth.

His vigilance pays off, as he spots a Pigeon. Instantly he focuses on his next move, and he dives down at 200 mph to snatch the Pigeon out of mid air. The Pigeon, likely, never feels a thing because of the precision in this moment.

The Falcon ensures the quality of this moment, and the next moment by being completely focused. Living each single, precious, moment.

The Falcon has complete, absolute focus within this moment. Can you catch something at 200 mph and not get hurt? With the right equipment, and focus, yes. Without absolute focus, no.

The Falcon is relaxed, determined, poised, prepared, calm, full attention in the moment. The result is a full tummy, a meal for its chicks, self respect, self confidence (to use human terms). Only positives. Because of his living within each moment, he is ensuring the quality of the next moment, his future.

If the Falcon were not using universal time, not focused, you might hear something like this, "Gosh darn that pigeon was slippery, and my balance was off, just like yesterday. I wish I could hunt better. Now my kids are hungry, and I won't get a full paycheck, how will I pay the rent?".

Being in the moment, fully focused, the Falcon doesn't waste energy on any negatives. No dwelling on yesterday or dreading tomorrow. No excuses, no blaming.

You can be free of those things as well!

One positive action after another.

Efficient.

Effective.

Happy.

If he had missed the Pigeon, he would have found another thermal air pocket, and used it to lift him high in the sky once again. No delay due to self criticism. Just one positive action after another. The epidemy of efficiency, effectiveness, success, and happiness!

This moment right now, the Falcon puts out his best effort, the only kind he knows. Each moment has its own 'best' effort. Our best can vary from moment to moment, clearly due to so many circumstances. However, it is still 'best'! Success, true to form, is soon to follow. It is the ultimate of owning your life, your actions, your power. Once again, you are in a position to make a choice. Choose this!

Me, I live within the moment, this one, right now, and I feel your presence. All of us do. We want you to feel the comfort of universal time as it allows you to connect with your innate universal intelligence, your instincts.

> *In the space of this moment, you can live a lifetime.*

You will feel things more clearly, sensations will be stronger, everything is brighter, fresher, calm, exciting, vivid. Use the alarm clock, or clock time when you must, it's simply a resource. That's ok.

In the space of this moment you can live a lifetime.

It's your moment, it's your life! When you choose to live within the moment, to find your happy, enhanced with the quality of your attention, you will feel and be alive!

-Darling

Are you a spectator in your life?

In that case, everyone and
everything else
are making all the choices,
including yours.

Get into the game, it's your life to dream, to live!

~Me

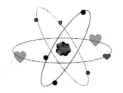

The Sixth Observation
<u>I'm Feeling It!</u>

Feelings are meaningful ways the body communicates the truth of what is happening, allowing us opportunity to sincerely effect our well being, our happiness.

Hello y'all. My name is Mason, my friends all call me Red, and I'm a Unity Rock. I'm the sixth stepping stone, so to speak in this lil' book!

How do you feel today? I ask, in all sincerity, because I care. Also, because my Observation is all about feelings. Beautiful, amazing feelings, like a Rose. Yet, feelings without pain, so thornless. Now you see a little of why I am called the North American Red Thornless with Feeling.

My Observation is that for you, the human, feelings are quite often associated with pain. So much so, that avoiding feelings becomes the objective.

A lot of work goes into y'all not feeling stuff. It's like a voluntary disconnect from feeling, often using food, drugs, alcohol, money, work, anything at all as a buffer.

This is not the 'norm' in nature. In nature, feelings are useful, meaningful, ways the body communicates the truth of what is happening for us. Our feelings are an integral part of making choices that will impact us immediately. So they are not something we want to blur.

In nature, if we 'feel' fearful, we notice. The faster we figure it out, the sooner we can respond. So we spend fractions of 'time' feeling it, because it is acted on immediately and positively.

A dog crossing the street, hears a sound that alerts him to possible danger. He springs into action. The time it takes from hearing to acting is almost indiscernible. The dog has trust for his feelings, listens to them, and confidence to act on them. He lives another day, because he feels.

"I'm Mason, I'm often taken for Granite. Like feelings are often taken for granted. Ha!"

-Red

My Observation comes down to this, You will feel. I feel. We don't change our physiological function of being able to feel, because that is natural, it is universal wisdom installed in you, in me. What we do is choose to listen to our feelings. To appreciate how meaningful and valuable their message is. Then act in a wise, effective way to create and ensure the quality of your 'self', your living.

A beautiful secondary benefit, is you will feel less pain as you develop this natural ability. Your life will become thornless, you will be the flower, in all your glory!

You will experience less pain in your life as you cultivate a natural relationship with your feelings.

I'm an interesting rock in bringing this subject up. I'm Red Granite. Often I am taken for granted, ('granite' haha!). Granite, is a very common rock, actually we are all quite common, but as it seems, on a volume scale, Granite is quite common. I am as prolific as feelings.

As Red Granite, I usually have some Quartz and Feldspar in me. I have layers, and I'm colorful! My pinks, reds, earth tones, all play nicely together!

Some say that Granite is a great perspective enhancer. What I mean is, I help bring the bigger picture into focus. I have a knack for it.

Granite can also help as a balancing agent for relationships and diplomacy. Like a tight rope walker uses a long pole to help keep their balance high up on a wire. I'm a tool, for helping you feel, and balance out your feelings, with reason, perspective, appreciation, determination.

Lets pause for a moment, and take our time to connect.

Breathe in, feel the temperature of the air as you inhale. Put your hand in front of your mouth when you exhale. Your breath is warm, nice, humid. Relax your arms, shoulders, fingers, and breathe in again, deeply. Saturate your lungs, your blood with air, oxygen, love. Mmmmmmm, yum.

Breathe.

Think more clearly as a result. Give your 'self' every opportunity to feel wonderful!

Think clearly. Happily. Hi again!

So, as I mentioned, feelings are a physiological fact. Not to be dismissed. Part of the natural function in all of nature.
This is not a powerless reality. This is not to say you are a 'victim' to your feelings and emotions.

This is important to understand. Often you will hear comments like "I can't help it..;" or "You are making me so mad."

Those type of comments are typical of a false understanding of feelings. A belief that you don't have any control over your feelings when things happen. You simply have to endure or enjoy whatever comes. Like a roller coaster ride!

> *Feelings are not a powerless reality combined with knee jerk reactions.*

Not so. There are choices for you to make. You are not powerless. You are able to train your 'self'.

Truth, according to nature is, that you choose your feelings. You can actively choose how to feel and then act. Reducing, and eliminating reflexive actions! Stay with me now, I know there are many situations, many types of feelings, just hear me out!

It is about choosing what to feel. As soon as you recognize a feeling, you are now in the drivers seat. It's wonderful. A powerful contrast to feeling miserably subject to whatever may come.

Let me use an example.

Start by noticing that when you listen to a song and you start to feel sad, the music and lyrics are set up to tell a sad story, you might even begin to cry. Then you decide, "Wait, I don't want to cry! My make-up will get ruined!" or your sinuses will get clogged! So you change the station, and find something else, that is upbeat, and the sad goes away.

Interesting! That is an example of identifying what you are feeling and choosing to feel something else.

The Universe, and you, know that your body is incredibly smart. It is also completely trusting. It's not that you are a body and a mind. Separate things. It's that you are a cooperation of mind and body. (Even more than that!)

Notice what you 'input' creates feelings.

You control the input.

Own the remote!

Think about it, your body knows hot and cold and reacts accordingly. That is the more absolute physical response. Your body can handle that without much interpretation. Like stubbing your toe. However, your body relies on you, as you take in images, music, conversation, complex things that involve multiple senses, it trusts you to control the input and to direct it.

It trusts you and what you tell it. What you think it believes. What you dream it feels! This makes you the 'adult', the responsible entity for your body (the 'child'), it's well being.

> *Your body trusts you completely, and provides you a genuine response to the input received.*

When you watch a movie, the story, the music, the characters, you take all of that in, and it evokes a reaction. Happy, sad, devastated, depressed, lonely, stressed... Guess what? Your body doesn't know that the movie isn't real. Your mind, the 'adult' does. Your body is trusting your eyes, ears, heart, mind, and it feels. This is why you can feel so exhausted when leaving the theater, or so happy and energized! This is why you wake up from a dream soaked in fearful sweat. Your body was living that dream. It was real, it felt real.

Your body is like a small child, you are holding it's hand and leading your body through each moment of each day. It needs you to give it your attention, and notice what you are feeling.

As your body responds to the feelings, you get to choose if it's good for you, and what you need to do actively to ensure the quality of your little 'self'.

This is your privilege, to protect and nurture your human body.

Like a Goldfish that can eat non-stop until it dies from overeating, the human body needs you to set limits on how much feeling it will experience. Too much and you get sick, even die.

You can feel wonderful and positive just by the first step of paying attention and feeling! Then take a positive action. It may not change what is happening completely, or right away. That's ok. Each of these decisive actions add up, and become exponentially significant.

You can feel wonderful just by giving your 'self' and what you are feeling some love and attention.

By choosing to be connected to the positive of Love, Happiness, Generosity, your connection to the Universe, to this moment, you can reduce the physical symptoms that the body often endures from too much stimuli.

The other type of feeling, that you are more accustomed to setting limits with are tangible feelings, the more absolute physical feelings. Like a hot flame touching your skin, or a full bladder calling for a bathroom. That's a little easier to identify, but the other, the emotional stuff, that requires practice.

Each day you are faced with gagillions of decisive moments. An upsetting video clip, memories from a child hood trauma, an abusive relationship, gossip at work or on your phone, all these things will replay in your mind over and over.

> *Practice self talk.*
> *When you go to the bathroom, say, "Thank you, this is a good idea. I feel much better. Smile. Feel your happy.*

Will you choose to allow this?

Choose to identify what you feel. What are you experiencing? Fear? Anxiety? Depression?

If it was a small child watching the movie you have in your head, you wouldn't let them watch. You would protect them. Shield them. This is exactly what you must do for your body! Protect your little 'self'! This is you taking your attention away from the negative. This is a powerful action.

You won't miss the gore. The drama. The drain on you physically and emotionally. As you get more and more adept at 'changing the station' so to speak, you'll see how wonderfully peaceful and empowering it is. It creates smiles!

Sometimes you have to physically remove yourself from someone, something. That's ok. Only you can protect your little childlike, trusting, body. In return your body will show appreciation! You will feel better, sleep better, feel healthier, more alert, clear, happier, hopeful, productive, grateful.

Your body, all of you, have the ability within to handle any 'thing', any event.

Trust your 'self'.

Your feelings will no longer be the enemy!
No longer will you choose to create the unmanageable pain, pain that has taken many, many lives in despair.

Live thornless, with feelings. Not creating pain for you. Not creating pain for others.

Situations do happen that are unforeseen, that do require us to react, to behave spontaneously, or that may even be horrific. However, the habit of choosing your emotions and safeguarding your body will only help you through these events.

You cannot diffuse a fear without facing it.

Ask your 'self', "What am I afraid of?"

The simple act of facing your fear, your feelings, will enable you to act with thoughtful intent.

When you feel fear, panic, anxiety… notice that you are probably thinking in another time zone, in the future. Usually about things that haven't happened yet, that aren't real. But your body is still feeling it!

There is always a positive action to be taken, in this very moment you are feeling this anxiety.

Start by giving yourself a little pat on the back for noticing what you are doing. Then, even if it doesn't seem related to helping the future anxious event, find something positive to do. Brushing your teeth. Folding clothes. Do a few dishes. Make a bed. Pat the dog!

Choose a positive action and feel the moment that you are in. The dog appreciates your love and attention, smile, and give him that moment fully. You can choose to feel this!

You can find little things to do now that will ensure that future moment goes as well as possible given your choices. Trust your body, act now.

Actively affecting your feelings ensures the quality of that future moment, and this moment!

What about depression? Feeling guilt, remorse, apathy, depressed? Is your mind in the past? Your body is feeling it NOW! Give your 'self' kudos for noticing! Loving your 'self' with a little attention!

A forest begins to regrow after a fire.

No second thoughts.

No delay.

Simple positive action.

Start with consciously telling yourself, "Good Job me! I noticed how we are feeling!"

Now, find something you can do, right now, something active, to help you change the feeling into a productive, positive feeling of good!

Give your cat a kiss! Clean the toilet! Do a math problem. Take a shower. Whatever you do, try to practice staying out of the old feeling, and feeling what you are actively doing. Feeling the good in it!

You know how to 'change the station'!
All of nature, in its infinite wisdom practices this balance.

> *"We may appear to be more simple than a human, but perhaps we have just chosen differently."*
>
> *-Red*

A bird may lose a chick to a storm yet, begins to rebuild, lays more eggs. An animal may survive a nightmare situation, yet still has the heart to give and love, leaving the scars in the past. A cat will sense a danger and move her kittens, not losing time to ineffectual panic or indecision. A forest begins to regrow after a fire, no second thoughts, no delay.

The sun rises each day with deliberate intent.

All around, the planet makes choices constantly. It goes through life and death, but not drama. It faces obstacles, but not overwhelmed. It learns through experience, but not with guilt or regret.

The planet is paying attention, clear, in the moment, strong, positive, grateful, happy. It feels. We truly do. We may appear to be more 'simple' than humans, but perhaps we have just chosen differently.

This is your life. Your choices. Gift your 'self' this attention! Feel this moment you are in!

Each time you pay attention, you notice your feelings, they are acknowledged.
Real.
Valid.
How long you choose to feel the present feelings is your choice. Actively pay attention and choose. Choose what to feel, and reinforce it with a positive action! Stay focussed in the moment, you will be given back whatever you need in that moment.
This is a universal provision, the proof is all around you, in abundance!

Get used to the power of your choices! It is wonderful!

-Red

Look in the mirror,
look deeply into your own eyes,
smile at your self,
ask your self,
"What can I do to make You Happy?"
Listen to your body!
What are you feeling?
Choose to respond with love towards your little 'self".

(Paraphrased Louise Hay and Blade.)

The Seventh Observation
<u>Chew the Fat! (cew!)</u>

Appreciate the value and enormous power of your words for creating good, moment by moment, for your 'self' and all others.

Hi hi! My name is Brook, and I am one of the African Purple Amethyst, with Breath.

I have a very important subject it is my privilege to discuss. While I may be the seventh, and final Observation, all of these Observations were brought to you via the power of words. Communication.

My Observation is on the power of words, written and spoken. When we appreciate and respect how important our communication is, we encourage the positive energies throughout our lives, the Planet, the Universe!

Our goal is to reduce the division that happens among all of us, and our communication is the 'iceberg'. Often not seen as the huge force that it is.

The every day, every moment words you use to communicate, either create wonderful, clear, positive energy, or contribute to the 'dark side'!

Let me introduce myself briefly, as the rock that I am. I am raw, genuine Amethyst. I have clear, purples, blues, and earth tones that characterize my appearance. I have been told, that stones, rocks, in their most natural state are very powerful.

> *Appreciation and respect for the power in communication and the ability to create good, moment by moment, within all the Universe.*

Do you agree?
I have also been told that the Amethyst has a direct link to the mind. So, for instance, if you touch me, we communicate well. (Non-verbal, by the way! hah!) I also help clear your thoughts, keep focus, and encourage realistic thinking patterns.

I love the part about how Amethyst can help with recalling dreams, and being content.
I help quiet the mind.
These are things humans have told me they feel. I know rocks are very powerful, so no doubt it is their truth.

My focus is on helping you to be able to communicate with me, and others of course! Does that mean you will be able to talk to me, or any little rock, and they will respond? Heh, well, let me know if that happens will ya?

We want communication that draws us closer together, creating a more powerful positive whole. Remember our end goal is to reduce the things that create division or separation on the planet.

We all benefit from thoughtful, meaningful communication patterns.

Communication happens with every thing. Even a rock. Yes. I said it. Energy communicates.

For example, the sun sends wonderful energy to the planet, you can feel its warmth on your skin, smile, it's nice. That feeling is communicated, like sun kisses. However, too much time in the sun, and your skin tells you, by its color and feel that you are burned. Sun burn is a communication.

> *Communication when thoughtful and meaningful, draws us closer, creating a more powerful whole.*

Then there is the active verbal communications going on constantly. A cat meows, purrs, hisses, spits, all with meaning. The dog barks, growls, whines, all with intent, meaning.
Communication.

What about you?

Your communication whether you have given it thought, has meaning, intent, results. It can be a powerful force for uniting or for creating division. It is so powerful that words, and their impact can lie within you for your entire life. In an ongoing way, affecting you and others.

My Observation is on appreciating the value of your words. I show how nature communicates, and why nature has less issues.

Nature uses a simple communication style that encourages respect and trust.

To start it is good to understand that Nature doesn't use words that are called 'descriptives'.

Humans use lots of descriptive words, that can be very useful. For instance, "On the left side of that blue car is a black cat."

That is nice and clear, right?

Seems like a very simple sentence. No judgement, no right, no wrong. Yet, watch what can happen.

Now, I just mentioned a black cat and if you associate a "black" cat with superstition and evil, then now the cat is bad. It was supposed to be a simple color, but then it got complicated. This is an example of how different ways we can communicate can have a variety of effects.

Descriptive words in particular, can create issue, can be divisive. True you cannot control or dictate how another will choose to interpret your words. However, nature, the Universe, tends to communicate without the complexity of the many descriptive terms that often create issues. So, it's nice for you to take this moment and perhaps understand a little bit about Universal communication!

The Universe is simple, true, honest. No subtle undertones, no assumptions, no guess work, no exaggeration.

In Nature what is said is simply what is.

Truth.

Honest.

Effective.

What is said is simply what it is.

For instance a bird sends out a warning call, and all the other birds know of danger. They act accordingly. There is no judgement on what is the danger, that would slow down their reaction.

There is no argument as to if it is truly a danger. Because there is no lying, no false words, so to speak. Only truth, honest, simple.

One way to keep it simple is done by not using very many descriptive type words. If I see something and it is kind to my eyes, I like what I am seeing. I can say simply "That's nice."

Seriously, if I saw that same black cat I mentioned earlier, I would simply say, "Nice."

Simple statements allow the other to observe, feel, 'see' for themselves.

It is a form of trust.

While subtle, here's what makes that simple statement so powerful. For humans they usually say something "is..." followed by a bunch of explaining stuff. Try stopping right there. That is. I am. Just be.

Whatever the 'it' that is being observed, it could be a feeling, situation, a flower, a dress, a poem. Whatever would come after the 'is' remains unspoken, yet understood as only each individual can and will understand.

No worries, there are lots of times when you will elaborate. This method of communication is not 'less than' because of the absence of elaboration! Instead, it can even be more meaningful and intense. Here is why.

The one receiving this comment will observe and what 'is' takes shape for them.

Their perception.

No one else.

This will happen anyway.

No matter how hard you try to communicate clearly, the other person will still have their own perception. Which is the beauty of being an individual.

Practice taking the time to absorb what another says, before responding.

Truly listen with all of your 'self'.

When the bird sent out the warning call, he didn't have to identify it was a Blue Tail Hawk. The other birds had time to react, get to safety, and observe for themselves.

When we allow others to observe for themselves, they have valuable observations, and it can enrich the experience for both parties.

It encourages trust, confidence, kindness, love,...

Try using less descriptives, and allow for the other person to absorb and appreciate. Less is said, yet more communication happens.

It's like creating a space, an open area that is available for each person to fill with their own stuff.

> *Natural communication is a very confident way to communicate. Powerful, effective, respectful.*

What's kinda funny is that Humans think that if they don't share what comes after the 'is' that everything will be quiet. Conversation will be stilted.

That can happen, especially if someone thinks you simply lost your thought. That's ok. People quickly catch on to others style, or methods of communication. It is interesting, different, creative.

It takes practice, but it is a very confident way to communicate. Powerful. Effective. It is also respectful. We all have our own thoughts, and we are allowing each to have theirs, without judgement.

Shared or unshared each individuals thoughts are valid. Real. True for them.

'Old school' humans remember when they would watch a movie, and the movie didn't show many things on the screen that were 'happening'. They didn't have to.

You knew in your mind what was happening.

The bloody gore, serious intimacy, what was in the drawer, or behind the door, these things were left to the power of imagination.

No problem there! The human mind is powerfully capable.

> "Shared or unshared, each individuals thoughts, words, are valid, real, true for them."
>
> -Brook

Of course conversations with descriptives is fun, it's funny, it's dramatic, colorful, animated, wonderful, lazy, creative, hopeful, dreamy, idealistic....(this is fun!).

However, a very important point is that **disunity** can result from using descriptive words. This is what we are trying to avoid.

This happens when they impact human feelings, which they do quite often.

Most humans I have met remember things said to them, good and bad, from their earliest childhood throughout their entire life.

These memories, experiences add up, and are like baggage, then carried through life. This is all contained within your cells, your atoms!

> *Your words are the only words you can control.*
>
> *Once you embrace this reality, you can let go of trying to control others thoughts, feelings, actions, words.*
>
> *It's very freeing.*

It's like a heaviness within. It's uncomfortable, and unwanted. Notice how weighty these word associated memories can be, how much depression, guilt, grief they have. They have an affect on your body, your health, your efforts to move forward with your life.

You likely wouldn't mind giving those negatives up! Part of giving them up, is learning to not create more.

Stopping a pattern of unhealthful communication can reliably be done one way. It stops with you. Your words are the only words you can control. Know that. Trust yourself.

Choose at times to not respond. Choose at times to not tell a story that will unnecessarily create anger, sadness, or bad feelings. You can decide to end the power those words have by not saying them!

This is a powerful action, and takes some practice! However, the end result is often very satisfying. For instance, you can be among family, and enjoying a nice meal when you remember something that happened at school or work.

As you get ready to relate the story, you realize it will make your brother angry, and he will likely react. This will change the entire pleasant mood at the dinner table. You also know that telling the story won't benefit anyone at that moment.

Use your words to actively, consciously, create good.

Happiness.

It can wait, if and when it even needs to be told. Instead you can choose to find something more interesting, positive, creative to discuss.

Sometimes, this presents a nice opportunity to listen to others more fully. You end up bringing more meaning to the life and conversations going on by censoring out the negative.

Learning when to bring up something, is as important as how it is brought up. Use your words to actively create good.

Leave out anger, or other emotions. Simply relate the truth. Like the birds warning call. Effective. Loving.

Most conversations will happen with a much better result by waiting for the right time. Then, by leaving out anger, or other emotions, simply relating the truth. Just like the birds warning call. No drama. Just the truth. No exaggeration.

No matter what needs to be discussed, keep your goal in front of you, to actively create good with your words. You will be able to finish a conversation happy. Satisfied not too much had to be said, just enough to be meaningful.
Less is more.

Practicing this Universally natural way to communicate, is very closely related to the simple art of listening.

There is a joy involved in true listening, that you can experience because you suddenly realize this is what you appreciate, when someone is truly hearing you! They don't interrupt. You can see in their eyes that they are not thinking of what they want to say. You can feel they understand as best they can. They don't hold this against you. They don't judge you.

They appreciate the true inherent freedom you have as a person, to speak freely. They are truly sharing this moment with you.

In response you can appreciate being heard. You don't look for them to fix anything. If you want their feedback or opinion you have the freedom to ask for it. Allowing for you to then listen to them with the same meaningful attention.

You create an environment around you where others feel heard.

Appreciated.

Understood.

Nice.

It is called 'active' listening. It takes effort to close the mouth and open the ears, to cease the mind talk while listening, and to truly embrace what you hear.

Leaving judgement and opinion out.

Now, practice this with even more vigilance when listening to your 'self'! Your inner voices. These voices are incredibly powerful. When you can hear your 'self' you will be able to know your 'self' and act on your behalf. It's a huge part of communication with all aspects, relationships, people, nature, in the course of your life.

Create the environment within you as well.

A place where you feel heard, appreciated, loved, happy!

Listening to your 'self' is often best done when you combine it with a breathing exercise. It helps to give yourself a little cushion of space, a place to actually have nothing be. Just long enough to help you to reconnect with you.

Imagine in your minds eyes, you sitting on a couch. Sitting next to you, is you.
A little you. You as a child. Can you remember what you looked like at the age of 6 or 8? Find a picture if you can, make the visual image real, after all it is real, it is you.

Your feet don't touch the floor, you laugh easily, you move without pain or effort. Your hair is tousled, or smooth, wild...

You look into your own eyes, see the childlike trust in your eyes. The wonder, the enthusiasm, the heart? Imagine feeling yourself reaching over, and taking your little hand. It is soft, gentle, warm.

This is you, the little 'self', the inner child as you are often called. This is the forever you. The eternal you. Perfect, teachable, loving, generous, kind, happy! Imagine a kitten or a puppy at the most adorable perfect age, that is what you are! That adorable, innocent, beautiful!

> *Your little 'self' is the forever you. Eternal, perfect, teachable, loving, happy!*

This little you goes through everything that you go through in your moment to moment.

Your little 'self' needs you. They still feel things like a little child. They don't have your experience, and understanding of what all is going on. Your little 'self' needs you to treat them like the little 'self', like a child, and to take care of them, make them feel safe, cared for, loved.

When you feel fear, this is the little 'self' expressing what they are feeling. When you feel anything, your little 'self' needs attention. The more you can create and nurture this relationship, the more confident and healthy you will be. Moving forward in life, in relationships, at school, your goals, work, fun stuff, everything, will be more connected.

Connect often through your day with your little 'self'.

Nurture this time with breath.

You will feel the difference! This is the feeling of being united within your 'self' even more. It's wonderful. It is a beautiful symbiotic relationship.

Take this time to connect with your little 'self', and breathe through this moment!
Remember, smiling creates deeper breathing. Smile at your 'self'.

Close your eyes, imagine you as an innocent, sweet, healthy, little person, puppy, or kitten! That little you is there. Waiting, hopeful, maybe nervous, scared, but happy, and excited!

It's ok. Talk to your little 'self'. Out loud is even better sometimes.
Tell your little 'self', "I love you. I will always protect you."
Try this now, take a nice deep breath together.

Give your full attention to your breath.

It will be impossible to think about anything else.

The breath will create a cushion of space, in time, in your space...

If you are still thinking of 'things' the you are not entirely focussed on your breathing. Keep trying! Listen to your breath sounds, feel the happy.

Now let it out fully.

More fully.

Try again.

Keep practicing this and increasing the depth of the breaths. At the moment when you have let all the air out, turn your attention to how you feel, deep down in your tummy, in your gut. What do you feel? This may be what your little 'self' is feeling.

As your little 'self' gains confidence, their voice will become louder, stronger, more confident.

That breath made just enough space so that you can feel, truly feel whatever is going on. There may be a little voice there. A tiny, almost inaudible voice. This is the little 'self' trying to speak up. Practice listening for your little voice. As your little 'self' gains confidence, the voice will become louder, stronger, more confident.

Sometimes it's a surprise. Like, "Wow, I need to go to the bathroom." or "Huh, I'm angry."

Sometimes it's nothing at all.

You may have to re-aquaint your 'self' with a new feeling, that of truly being happy!

Nice.

Content.

Good.

Happy.

Breathe!

You may have to get used to a new feeling! The happy feeling of your 'self' humming happily, contentedly, coloring, smiling, safe.

Knowing you, all of you, is being cared for. Loved.

If you find your 'self' kinda suffering, your thoughts spinning, or your body not clear, that's ok. There are no rules here. Your body, your little 'self', is simply trying to communicate with you, and that can take time, practice, patience, love.

Breathe!

Try to remember some of your early feelings as a child, this connection will be like reawakening to your thought processes as a child. Those are all still within you, dormant in many cases. It can be in a way like learning a language you used to speak. Think of it as fun, exciting, a part of you being welcomed back into your day to day, moment by moment world. Now the two of you will face those moments, feeling together, and being there for the other.

This is the internal support system within you, always there, simply waiting to be welcomed back onto the playground of your life.

Be aware of your breath!

Give your little 'self', and your big 'self' some kudos for trying to connect, and keep trying. Look into the mirror, into your eyes, and use your breathing to help you, tell your 'self', "Let's be happy!". Use your words out loud to help make this experience more real, and give it more impact! It is surprisingly effective! Smile!

Imagine a puppy all excited to see you, the irrepressible joy and happiness, this is your little happy 'self'!

This is a way of thinking, feeling, communicating with your entire body, in all its complexity.

If ever you don't know what to do, don't know what you want, confused, indecisive, practice your breathing! Remind your 'self', those feelings don't have the power to dictate your life. They are important. Tell your 'self' a little thank you in essence for sharing, and then breathe again.

Then choose something, anything, positive, to do that will create action. Nothing happens when you are indecisive. Just trust yourself, move forward, choose as best you can in this moment. Breathe!

> *Move past feelings by appreciating their being valid, and then act positively in any way you find!*

This kind of breathing is also called 'following your breath'. Envision your breathe, the happy power within.
Practice often, anywhere, anytime.
In the kitchen, standing in front of the fridge, in front of the mirror, lying in bed, in the car, at your desk, in the yard, mute the commercial and breathe! In time, this practice can create a sense of peacefulness. A still, quiet happy place within your 'self'.
Sometimes bad feelings feel like they dominate. Like they are eating you alive, day in and out. You can choose to affect it.
Choose to feel something else. Just like Red talked about in the Sixth Observation!

You can. It's not bigger than you. **You** are the boss now. You are the protector of your little and big 'self.' Just like you are sitting at a table with friends, talking, and you can choose what to discuss, you can also choose what to think about.

It takes action. Action that will create your happiness!

Right now, your breath, with your attention, your full power, all this oxygen loving you, saturating your cells, every atom of you. This process of being aware of your communications internal and external, censoring out any negativity, you are slowing down, even stopping the taking on of further damage to your 'self'.

Practice is not required because of failure.

Practice is simply the art of learning. Training. Success.

This is also the perfect time to release some of that accumulated stuff you carry around.

One very effective way to release bad stuff, is that when it comes up you replace it with something else, something positive.

In life it seems much easier to replace things than to remove them.

A bird will not rebuild a nest that is too damaged, instead the bird will start fresh. A car that has been too damaged, will often be replaced. Memories that create negativity can be replaced. That is not the same as deleted, as though they didn't exist. Rather, when a recurring negative thought happens, you take a positive action and think of something else. You choose.

Instead of letting the pain of someone who is now gone from your life overcome you, focus on a happy moment with them, and feel that happiness again. Celebrate the life. The pain will not serve you. You can learn without pain.

You can learn without pain.

Appreciate the value of your words. Choose them with care. Creating no pain for you or others.

Thoughtful speech.

So, for instance, you remember someone yelling and saying horrible, hurtful things. This may evoke deep, emotional reactions, because the little 'self' still feels that as vividly as if it were happening right now. Your body feels it. The big 'self' must take action.

Choose your happy!

Communicate with your little and big 'self'. Comfort and reassure your little 'self' that now you will remember a positive thing. Create an arsenal of memories you can use to insert, or replace when the negative tries to rise up like a monster, trying to squash you.

You can think about that first smile you saw on your childs face. It may have been gas, but it was cute. Makes you smile! This is happy! You can see it vividly in your minds eye. The sweet, gentle nuzzle of a puppy on your cheek. Gratitude. Someone you love laughing so hard you all cry! Love. A beautiful sky. Puffy white clouds being lazy.

This is communication, appreciating the power of your thoughts, feelings, words.

Creating only good, moment by moment.

This is Happy.

Wonderful, powerful memories, full of thornless feelings as Red calls them! Call these replacement memories. Keep them close to you.

Find memories you can fill into these spaces, that make you smile, feel happy all over.

Create more of them,
and use them often.
This is communication. The
value of your words, your
thoughts, your feelings, the
little 'self', your big 'self',
all together, with all of us,
creating our happy.

We are.
You are.

Lets be.

-Brook

Happy.

Just a little bit...

Find Your Happy! is the wonderful result of my love for the Planet, as she inspires me each day!

Taking my life long appreciation for rocks to another level, and having them be the Teachers in this little book, is one way of showing my gratitude for the lessons I glean from Nature.

There are various ways to write, and share. My writing style is for the Adult-Child. It's almost simplistic, yet like Nature, takes complex matters and reveals them in their most simple form.

There are many who love this planet, and can appreciate that these seven rocks have a voice. That nature does observe us. That nature does have a voice. We can choose to listen, observe, and learn.

I am the accumulation of all who have touched my life, in person, through books, in endless ways. For over 40 years I studied from many varied faiths, always choosing to stay independent in one way or another. Always staying open, searching for further meaning, for things to make sense, purpose to be revealed.

Only Nature has had the answers to each question, providing the role models, and the courage to live true. Encouraging me to find my happy. To live it. Nature is my muse, and I love this planet!

There are many individuals to thank, who inspire me as well. From these individuals, things they have said, or written, I have created a list of affirmations that I use routinely. I'm sharing a few of them here. I hope you find them fun, familiar, and completely useful!

~Me

Some of My Personal Affirmations

I Love You.
Today begins anew, with
limitless possibilities, I am
connected to a universe of only good.
I live in abundance and gratitude.
I am open to change, new
experiences, and adventure.
I am loving, courageous, and brave.
I do what is front of me,
and ride the wave of opportunity.
I have plenty of everything I need.
My body and feelings are
my dearest friends and companions.
I am free of internal obstructions.
My mind is clear, my

emotions open, my body is elastic.
Like a tree, I move with the
forces of life.
Failure and success are
stepping stones towards my goals.
I realistically asses my
challenges, I prepare and
strategically manage my success.
My career is full of
creativity, laughter, and abundance.
I am motivated by love.
My goals give me the
power and discipline to go
through difficult transitions.
Less is more.
I appreciate each bite of
food as it nourishes and loves my body.
An aura of warmth and
authenticity surround me.

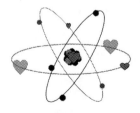

URthePlanet.com

Other Books by Constance Grace Stoner:

<u>Rock, Spider, Fly</u>

Raven is a young boy who overcomes his fear of spiders by learning to appreciate new friendships. Wonderful life experiences come as a result! Childrens/Adult book with colorful illustrations.

<u>Banditto, Living Free!</u>

This endearing little kitty, living free, and through his life course helps touch the hearts of his humans. Teaching his humans about being true to 'self'. Available in 2017. Childrens/Adult book with wonderful illustrations.

<u>I Am A Super Hero!</u>

The life journey for Bandit and Little Pebble leads them to discover the human concept of a Super Hero. They soon recognize how the Universe is nothing but Super Heros! Only the human species has yet to recognize and own their true powers! This is an Adult/Child book with illustrations, geared towards self empowered.

<u>Young Pebbles: How to Care for Your Unity Rock!</u>

Meet the Unity Rocks, as they share their world, and encourage each of us to connect with the planet, one rock at a time!

This
moment
matters,
it
determines
the
next
one.

Choose
love,
quality,
appreciation,
determination,

Happiness!

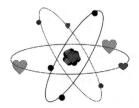

URthePlanet.com

Printed in the United States
By Bookmasters